DATE DUE

DEMCO, INC. 38-2931

THE
VIKINGS

Jason Hook

Thomson Learning • New York

Look into the Past

The Aztecs
The Egyptians
The Greeks
The Romans
The Saxons
The Vikings

First published in the
United States in 1993 by
Thomson Learning
115 Fifth Avenue
New York, NY 10003

First published in 1993 by Wayland (Publishers) Ltd.

Copyright © 1993 Wayland (Publishers) Ltd.

U.S. version copyright © 1993 Thomson Learning

Cataloging-in-Publication Data applied for

ISBN 1-56847-060-6

Printed in Italy

Picture acknowledgments
The publishers wish to thank the following for providing the photographs for this book: Ancient Art and Architecture Collection 11 (top): British Library 27 (right): C.M. Dixon 6, 7 (bottom, Ashmolean Museum, Oxford), 10 (right, Museum of National Antiquities, Stockholm), 11 (bottom), 13 (top, Museum of National Antiquities, Stockholm), 15 (both; right University Historical Museum, Oslo), 16, 17 (bottom), 19 (top, National Museum, Copenhagen; left), 21 (bottom left and top right, Viking Ship Museum, Bygdoy), 23 (both, Museum of National Antiquities, Stockholm), 23 (both, Museum of National Antiquities, Stockholm), 24 (British Museum), 29 (bottom); E.T. Archive 27 (left, Bodleian Library); Werner Forman Archive 5 (top), 6 (Statens Historiska Museum, Stockholm), 7 (top, Stofnun Arna Magnussonar a Islandi, Iceland), 8 (Universitets Oldsaksamling, Oslo), 9 (both, top Statens Historiska Museum, Stockholm, bottom, Viking Ship Museum, Bygdoy), 12, 14 (left), 18 (Statens Historiska Museum, Stockholm), 20 (Viking Ship Museum, Bygdoy), 21 (top left, Viking Ship Museum, Bygdoy), 22 (Statens Historiska Museum, Stockholm), 25 (right, National Museum, Copenhagen), 26 (both, British Museum), 29 (top); Michael Holford 25 (left, Staten Historiska Museum, Stockholm), 28 (Musée de Bayeux); York Archaeological Trust 5 (bottom), 10 (left), 13 (bottom), 17 (top 3).
Map artwork on page 4 by Jenny Hughes.

CONTENTS

Words that appear in *bold italic* in the text are explained in the glossary on page 30.

WHO WERE THE VIKINGS?

More than one thousand years ago, a race of pirates, traders, explorers, and settlers swarmed across Europe with such fury that their influence is felt even today. They were the Vikings: fearless warriors who discovered new lands, founded cities, and invaded foreign countries. They were so successful that their language and descendants still survive in many countries today.

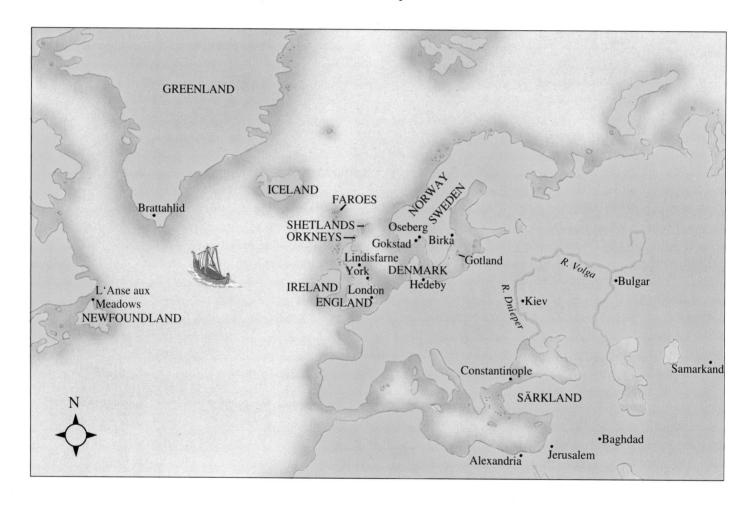

The name "Viking" describes the people who came from three countries of *Scandinavia* – Norway, Denmark, and Sweden – between A.D. 793 and A.D. 1066. This map shows how far the Vikings traveled on their many raids and voyages. Sailing east to Arab lands and west as far as America, the Vikings knew more of the world than anyone before them.

◀ In those days, it was quicker to travel by water than by land – across Sweden's many lakes, around the coasts of Denmark's five hundred islands, or along the deep, narrow **fjords** of Norway, like this one at Sogne. So, the Scandinavians had a long sailing **tradition**. When the population outgrew their farming lands, they sailed for foreign seas and the Viking Age began.

On June 8, 793, Vikings from Norway landed at Hold Island, off the coast of northeast England. They looted Lindisfarne monastery and killed its monks.
This ninth-century memorial stone shows these first Viking raiders. ▼

▲ **Archaeologists** have learned a lot about Vikings by studying **artifacts** found in areas where they lived. The Vikings buried weapons, jewelry, even entire ships with their dead, preserving important **relics** of their history. This carving from a cart buried in Oseberg, Norway, suggests the appearance of the Vikings whose raids terrorized Europe for some 250 years.

THE VIKING LANGUAGE

The Vikings spoke a language called Old Norse. Some modern towns have names formed from Norse words, showing that they grew from Viking settlements. The word "by" is Norse for "town." So, in England, the place-name "Danby" originally meant "Dane town," and the word "bylaw" means "law of the town." English words like "them," "take," and "die" are also of Viking origin.

Having no pens or paper, the Vikings carved thin letters called runes into wood and stone. Using two 16-rune alphabets called the futharks, they carved tombstones and jewelry with words that can still be read today. This stone shows the pre-Viking futhark of 24 runes.

Rune stones were put up to mark graves and bridges throughout the Viking world. This eleventh-century stone from Uppland, Sweden, reads: "Torsten caused this monument to be made in memory of Sven, his father, and of Tore, his brother, who were in Greece, and of Ingletora, his mother." Rune stones like this one, and the places where they have been found, show us how widely the Vikings traveled. ▼

▲ The sagas are another source of Viking history. They are tales based on real Viking adventures, which were beautifully handwritten in thirteenth-century Iceland. This picture from the Saga of St. Olaf shows the death of Olaf II Haraldsson, or Olaf the Stout, king of Norway from 1016 to 1028. Olaf, who forced his people to adopt Christianity, became patron saint of Scandinavia.

7

THE LONGSHIP

The Vikings became masters of the seas by building the finest ships of the time. With *keels* to steady them, Viking longships could sail swiftly across the open sea or be rowed into the shallowest waters. No one was safe from a sudden Viking attack.

Some longships had carved **figureheads.** Can you imagine what the figurehead would have been on a ship named "Long Serpent" or "Great Dragon"? Other ships had bronze **vanes** like this one, which later became a weather vane on Heggen Church in Norway. Dragon shapes are engraved on it. The dents are thought to have been caused by flying arrows.

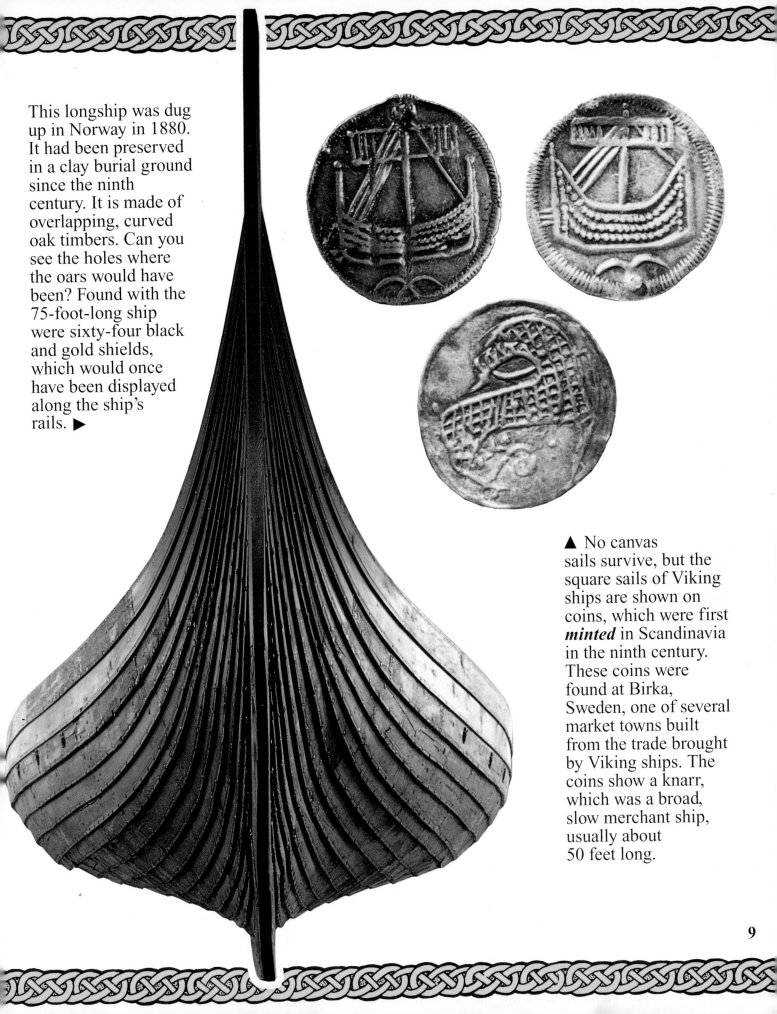

This longship was dug up in Norway in 1880. It had been preserved in a clay burial ground since the ninth century. It is made of overlapping, curved oak timbers. Can you see the holes where the oars would have been? Found with the 75-foot-long ship were sixty-four black and gold shields, which would once have been displayed along the ship's rails. ▶

▲ No canvas sails survive, but the square sails of Viking ships are shown on coins, which were first *minted* in Scandinavia in the ninth century. These coins were found at Birka, Sweden, one of several market towns built from the trade brought by Viking ships. The coins show a knarr, which was a broad, slow merchant ship, usually about 50 feet long.

TRADE

Vikings were raiders, but they also traded peacefully with distant *empires*. Trade created Scandinavia's first towns, like Birka, where archaeologists now find buried hoards of foreign silks, glass, and precious metals.

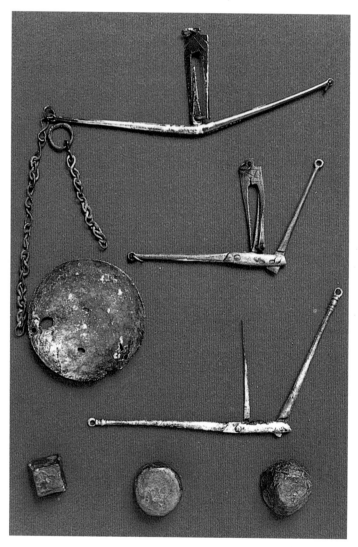

Swedish merchants sailed down the Volga and Dnieper rivers through Russia to the Black, Caspian, and Mediterranean seas. They ruled over Kiev and became known as the "Rus" – after which Russia is named. These Vikings traded furs, iron, wax, honey, even slaves, for Chinese silk and treasured Arabian silver. Eighty-five thousand Arabic coins like these have been dug up in Scandinavia, revealing the dates and sources of Viking trade. ▼

▲ Early Viking merchants did not give coins different values as we do today. They measured them purely by weight, using folding scales like these from tenth-century England. A trader might offer half a coin or a lump of silver chopped from a bracelet as change. Viking traders would close a sale by slapping hands.

◀ The collapse of the **Frankish Empire** after its powerful emperor Charlemagne died in 814 provided rich pickings for the Vikings. They traded and raided at the same time, taking home cloth, pottery, wine, weapons, and luxury items like this ninth-century silver cup found in Denmark.

International ▶ markets like Birka – where this tenth-century crucifix was found – attracted the first Christian **missionaries** and churches. Vikings often agreed to become Christians just so Christian merchants would trade with them.

SETTLERS

Viking ships boldly sailed from Norway, exploring west across the Atlantic. In 986 Vikings settled in Greenland. Then, according to the sagas, followers of Leif Eriksson – known as Leif the Lucky – landed in a place they named Vinland. Viking tools recently discovered at L'Anse aux Meadows, Newfoundland, show that Vinland was in America – the Vikings reached it five hundred years before Columbus.

The Vikings arrived in Iceland around 860. Glad to escape from the harsh rule of their king, Harald Fairhair, many of them settled there. When Leif Eriksson's father, Erik the Red, was banished from Iceland for murder, he voyaged even farther across the Atlantic. He discovered Greenland, and in 986 founded a colony that survived for five hundred years. Its remains, at Brattahlid, are shown here.

◄ Many Vikings traveled east in search of the fabulous wealth of Constantinople, the capital of the **Byzantine Empire.** Byzantine emperors formed the Vikings into their own personal army called the Varangian Guard. Rune stones like this one from Broby, Sweden, record the deaths of many Viking soldiers in the east: "Estrid had this stone erected in memory of Osten, her husband, who went to Jerusalem and died in Greece."

The rich farmlands of the United Kingdom encouraged the Viking raiders to settle down and form *colonies*. They settled in the islands off the coast of Scotland, in the Isle of Man, and in Ireland. In 867 they captured the city now called York, which they named Jorvik. This Viking boot was found there. Jorvik became the capital of the Viking kingdom ▼ of Northumbria.

THE VIKING PEOPLE

Most Vikings were landowners called bondirs or carls, who lived on family farms served by slaves called *thralls*. Above them were local chieftains called jarls or earls. The most powerful Vikings were the royal families of Denmark, Norway, and Sweden, the separate kingdoms in which Vikings lived.

A local assembly, called a ***Thing***, controlled law and order in each community. Vikings in Iceland formed Europe's earliest national parliament, the ***Althing***. This parliament met every year, here at Thingvellir, which means Parliament Plains. A lawgiver would mount the "law rock" to announce decisions, such as Iceland's conversion to Christianity in A.D. 1000. ▼

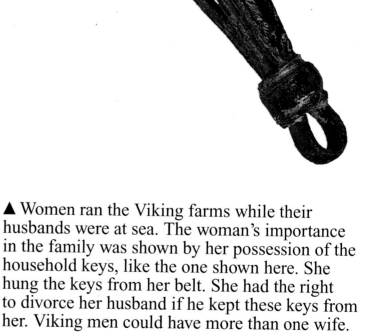

▲ Women ran the Viking farms while their husbands were at sea. The woman's importance in the family was shown by her possession of the household keys, like the one shown here. She hung the keys from her belt. She had the right to divorce her husband if he kept these keys from her. Viking men could have more than one wife.

Craftsmen such as carpenters and wood-carvers were highly respected in Viking society. These tools, which have modern handles, belonged to a Viking woodworker of Mästermyr, on Gotland. They would have been used for shipbuilding. ▼

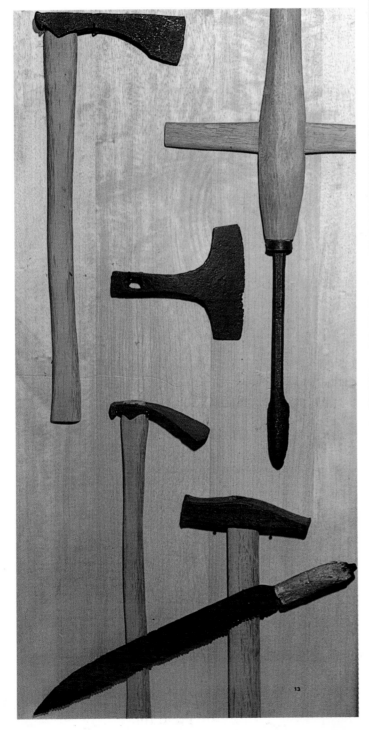

▲ The most valued craftsman was the blacksmith, who forged tools, weapons, nails, and locks, using the *anvil*, hammer, and tongs that today's smiths still use. This twelfth-century church carving illustrating the Viking *myth* of Sigurd the Dragon-Slayer shows Regin the Smith forging a sword strong enough to split his anvil.

DAILY LIFE

Archaeologists have discovered Viking remains of plowed fields, farm tools, animal bones, and even fishing tackle. These show that the Vikings were very efficient farmers, who could produce all the food they needed. They grew wheat and produced meat and dairy products. They also caught fish and wild animals to eat.

A typical family ate, slept, and worked in a single, rectangular hall or longhouse. Its walls were made of timber sealed with moss or wattle and daub (woven twigs covered with clay), and there were no windows. The house had a sloping roof that was thatched or turfed. Inside, sleeping benches ran along the walls, and a central hearth beneath a smoke hole supplied light, warmth, and heat for cooking. This is a reconstruction of houses and wooden paths at the Viking town of Hedeby in Denmark.

▲ The Vikings used wooden bowls, spoons and knives (but not forks), and many other kitchen utensils, like these from York, England. Their diet included fish and meat, which were salted and dried for long winters or sea voyages. They also ate cabbages, peas, oats, and fruits. Food was sweetened with honey, flavored by garlic and spices, and washed down with beer.

Every girl was ▶ taught to use a hand spindle. This was a weighted rod that spun thread from wool. The wool was dyed and woven on *looms* into cloth for clothing and sails. Linen, made from the flax plant, was smoothed on whale-bone "ironing boards" like this one.

APPEARANCE

In 922 an Arab trader named Ibn Fadlan wrote of Viking men's appearance: "I have never seen more perfect physical specimens, tall as date palms, blond and ruddy." Most wore beards parted in the middle, like the one that gave Danish king Svein Forkbeard his name.

Viking men commonly wore a belted, buttonless tunic under a cloak of fur or brightly dyed cloth. This was fastened at one shoulder by a ring-and-pin brooch, leaving the sword arm free. Trousers were either tight, like today's ski pants, flared, or very baggy. Men and women wore leather shoes, with hats and gloves of leather or wool.

This tenth-century brooch was discovered at Hornelund in Denmark. It shows the skill of Viking goldsmiths. The fine gold thread decoration is called filigree. Poorer people wore cheap copies of such jewelry, which were mass-produced. ▼

◄ To show off their wealth, Viking traders had silver coins melted down to make jewelry for their wives, like this beautiful bracelet from Denmark.

This Swedish pendant shows how a Viking ▶ woman dressed. She wore a long, pleated linen dress under two cloth rectangles hung from shoulder straps that were fastened by oval broaches. A shawl, held at the throat by a winged or drum-shaped brooch, was considered fashionable. Necklaces of glass beads were common. A married woman covered her hair with a head scarf.

19

BURIAL

The Vikings either *cremated* or buried their dead. They were buried with their finest possessions – for use in the afterlife. Many of these grave goods provide us with information about Viking life. Ships, so important in life, were believed to carry the dead to the next world. Gravestones were laid out in the shape of a ship. Kings and queens were buried beneath burial mounds containing slaughtered slaves and animals and entire longships.

The richest grave was discovered at Oseberg in 1904. It contained this beautiful 71-foot-long ship and the furniture of a royal household. Two skeletons found with it are possibly those of Queen Asa, grandmother of Harald Fairhair, and her *sacrificed* slave. Note the carved stern and the rudder or steer board, from which the word *starboard* comes.

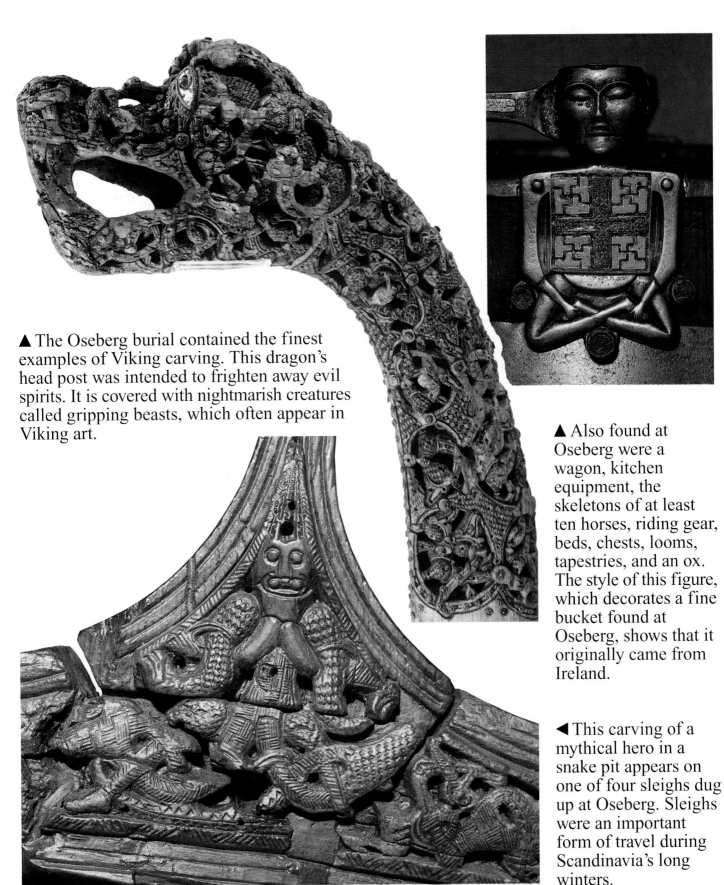

▲ The Oseberg burial contained the finest examples of Viking carving. This dragon's head post was intended to frighten away evil spirits. It is covered with nightmarish creatures called gripping beasts, which often appear in Viking art.

▲ Also found at Oseberg were a wagon, kitchen equipment, the skeletons of at least ten horses, riding gear, beds, chests, looms, tapestries, and an ox. The style of this figure, which decorates a fine bucket found at Oseberg, shows that it originally came from Ireland.

◄ This carving of a mythical hero in a snake pit appears on one of four sleighs dug up at Oseberg. Sleighs were an important form of travel during Scandinavia's long winters.

21

RELIGION

The Vikings followed an ancient religion. They worshiped a race of gods called the Aesir. Tales of the incredible adventures of these gods were told by generations of Viking poets called skalds and written down in the sagas of thirteenth-century Iceland.

Odin was the god of war and wisdom. His warrior-maidens, called *Valkyries*, chose the Viking warriors who would die heroically in battle and then led their spirits to Valhalla, the Hall of the Slain. Here they could fight all day and feast all night. The picture stone shows, top left, three slain warriors with their swords pointed down as they approach Valhalla. Odin's eight-legged horse, Sleipner, carries a fourth warrior.

Thor was the mighty, red-bearded thunder god. He fought with a magical hammer against his enemies, the Giants. Many Vikings carried charms like this tenth-century Thor's hammer to summon Thor's protection. Note the silver coils that represent Thor's staring eyes. The word "Thursday" originally meant "Thor's day." ▼

▲ This tapestry from a church in Sweden shows the three most important Viking gods (from left to right): the one-eyed Odin; Thor with his hammer; and Frey, god of *fertility*, holding an ear of corn. Human sacrifices were offered to these three gods at a Viking temple in Old Uppsala in Sweden.

WAR

The Vikings were most famous as warriors. They used weapons that were better than any that had been used before and followed a religion that encouraged them to be fearless. Vikings hated to die from old age – known as "a straw death." Dying in battle, however, offered the chance of going to glorious Valhalla.

Viking warriors did not wear the horned helmets often shown in movies. In fact, they wore plain, conical helmets – like the ones on these Norse chessmen from Lewis Island, Scotland. The figure biting his shield represents a *berserk*. This was a much-feared warrior who furiously attacked his enemies wearing no armor but a wolf or bearskin and howling like a beast. From this behavior comes the expression, "gone berserk."

Spears and bows ▶ were used, but the most popular weapon was the sword. Viking craftsmen added strong blades – traded from the Frankish Empire – to hilts of wood, horn, or precious metal. But, when the Vikings turned these deadly weapons against them, the Franks forbade their sale. Warriors gave their swords names like "Leg Biter" and "Golden Hilted," which might describe this weapon from Sweden.

▲ The deadly broad-bladed battle-ax was the symbol of Viking terror. Olaf the Stout named his ax "Hel" after the goddess of the dead. King Canute of Denmark allowed only axmen to join his bodyguard. This tenth-century iron ax head from Mammen in Denmark has a serpent design beautifully inlaid with silver.

THE INVADERS

By 870, Viking invaders had conquered most of England. Only Wessex, ruled by Alfred the Great, resisted them. Alfred signed a treaty called the Danelaw, giving the north of England to the Vikings. Similarly, in 911, King Charles III of France gave land to the giant Viking Rollo in return for Rollo's promise to become a Christian and to support the king. The land was called Normandy – Land of the Northmen.

When Aethelred became king of England in 978 he tried to buy peace by giving the Vikings payments of silver called *danegeld*. Such easy loot only encouraged Viking kings to return with larger armies. In 1016 Vikings received nearly 83,000 pounds of danegeld, including coins like these – one of which shows King Aethelred, who was called "Aethelred the Unready."

This is a page from the Anglo-Saxon Chronicles, in which English writers recorded the terror of "the force" – the Vikings. Even the nursery rhyme *London Bridge is falling down* recalls a Viking attack. In 1010 Olaf the Stout's oarsmen attached cables from their longships to London Bridge and dragged it down into the Thames. ▼

▲ In 1016 Canute Sveinsson, son of Svein Forkbeard, became the first Viking king of all England. Like many later Vikings, Canute was a Christian. He once commanded the ocean waves to turn back, to show that even a king was ruled by God. The waves kept coming, and Canute proved that only God is all-powerful. Canute died in 1035, having successfully ruled an empire including England, Denmark, Norway, and part of Sweden.

DOOMSDAY OF THE VIKINGS

The Vikings always believed the gods they worshiped would be destroyed at *"Ragnaök"* – "Doomsday of the Gods" – and that Odin would be eaten by his enemy, Fenris the Wolf. In fact, the downfall of their gods, and the end of the Viking Age, came with the spread of Christianity throughout Scandinavia.

In 1066 the last great Viking, Harold Hardraade, King Harold III of Norway, was defeated at Stamford Bridge by England's King Harold II – whose own last name, Godwinson, is a Viking one. Two days later, another Viking descendant, William of Normandy, invaded England. He crossed the Channel in the longships shown here on the ***Bayeux Tapestry*** and conquered England at the Battle of Hastings.

English rulers like William the Conqueror built up defenses and armies to end the great Viking raids. Vikings who had settled abroad were generally absorbed into the native population. Many reminders of the Viking Age remain, like this warrior laid out with his weapons for pagan burial, carved on a tenth-century cross at Middleton in Yorkshire, England.
▼

▲ Having once looted the Lindisfarne monastery, the Vikings then built their own churches, like this one at Borgund in Norway. It is called a stave church, after the upright planks or staves that construct its walls. As well as crosses, it is decorated with fierce dragon heads to scare away the old Viking gods.

GLOSSARY

Althing The national parliament of Iceland.

Anvil A heavy iron block on which metals are hammered into shape.

Archaeologist Someone who studies objects and remains from past civilizations.

Artifacts Objects, such as tools or pots, that archaeologists study to find out how people used to live.

Bayeux Tapestry A famous work of embroidery showing William the Conqueror's invasion of England.

Berserk Wild, fighting-mad warrior.

Byzantine Empire The Roman Empire in the East, whose capital was Constantinople.

Colony A settlement in a new country.

Cremate To burn a corpse.

Danegeld A tax in England that raised money to pay off Vikings.

Empire Foreign lands controlled by a country or emperor.

Fertility The ability of people to have children and of land to produce crops.

Figurehead Carving on the front of a ship.

Fjord A long, narrow sea inlet between high cliffs.

Frankish Empire The empire centered around Germany from about 400 to 850.

Keel The lowest beam of a ship, on which the rest of the ship's frame is built.

Looms Machines for weaving thread into cloth.

Mint To make metal into coins.

Missionaries Traveling religious preachers.

Myths Stories about heroes or gods and goddesses.

Ragnarök The predicted day of the Viking gods' destruction.

Relics Objects remaining from an earlier time.

Sacrifice To kill people or animals as offerings to a goddess or god.

Scandinavia Group name for Denmark, Norway, Sweden, and Iceland.

Starboard The right-hand side of a ship.

Thing Public lawmaking assembly of Vikings.

Thrall A Viking slave, who was not allowed to carry weapons.

Tradition A custom or practice passed on from one generation to another.

Valkyries Beautiful mythical maidens who served the god Oden by choosing the heroes to be slain in battle and taking them to Valhalla.

Vane A flat metal blade that shows which way the wind is blowing.

IMPORTANT DATES

793 Vikings raid Lindisfarne monastery on Holy Island in England
835 First Danish invasion of England
860 Vikings discover Iceland
867 York (Jorvik) in England captured by Vikings
886 Alfred the Great signs Peace of Wedmore, establishing Danelaw
911 Rollo receives Normandy from French King Charles the Simple
982 Erik the Red discovers Greenland
9840-1014 Svein Forkbeard reigns as king of Denmark
986 Leif Eriksson founds a colony in Greenland

995-1000 Olaf Tryggvason reigns as king of Norway
1000 Iceland adopts Christianity
1010 Olaf the Stout pulls down London Bridge
1016-1028 Olaf the Stout rules Norway
1016-1035 Canute rules as first Viking king of all England
1047-1066 Harold Hardraade reigns as king of Norway
1066 Harold Hardraade killed at Stamford Bridge; William of Normandy conquers England
1100s-1200s The sagas are recorded in Iceland

BOOKS TO READ

Caselli, Giovanni. *The Everyday Life of a Viking Settler*. New York: Peter Bedrick Books, 1991.

Costumes of the Saxons and Vikings. North Pomfret, VT: Trafalgar Square, 1991.

Humble, Richard. *The Age of Leif Eriksson*. Exploration Through the Ages. New York: Franklin Watts, 1989.

Mulvihill, Margaret. *Viking Longboats*. History Highlights. New York: Gloucester Press, 1991.

Triggs, Tony D. *Viking Warriors*. Beginning History. New York: Bookwright Press, 1991.

Matthews, Rupert. *Viking Explorers*. Beginning History. New York: Bookwright Press, 1990.

INDEX